AFTER THE CRASH

To: Jack Fletcher
My Classmate (1952 SCHS)

9/14/93

" Love Serber Webb"

AFTER THE CRASH

Rose Weite

P.O. BOX 26927 ❧ PHOENIX, ARIZONA 85068

AFTER THE CRASH
Copyright 1993 by Rose F. Weite

Library of Congress CIP Number 91-35708
ISBN: 0-9636043-0-9

CLEMENTINE BOOKS, INC./Publisher
Phoenix, Arizona 85068

Printed in the United States of America
First Edition

Library of Congress Cataloging in Publication Data:

      Weite, Rose F.
      After the crash / by Rose F. Weite
         p.   cm
      ISBN: 0-9636043-0-9
      1. Widowhood–United States–Case studies
      2. Bereavement–Psychological aspects
      3. Weite, Rose F.
      1. Title
      HQ1058.5U5W45   g1-35708
      306.88–dc20   CIP

AFTER THE CRASH

Acknowledgments

I SINCERELY THANK my family and friends for encouraging me to write this book.

Two special friends whom I cherish, Carole Nickleson and Connie Warren.

And a special thanks to Professor Norman Corwin and Greta Bishop, without whose help and encouragement I could never have written this book.

Dedication

I DEDICATE THIS book to my beloved husband, Len Weite, the passengers and crew of Northwest Flight 255, and their surviving families.

May we find peace at last and the courage to go on with our lives, secure in the knowledge that love is eternal, and beautiful memories last forever.

Rose Weite

August 16, 1987

A Northwest Airlines jet with 155 people aboard crashed just after take-off at Detroit Metropolitan Airport.

It struck several cars on the ground, and two people died when the truck in which they were riding was hit by the plane's wreckage.

Northwest Flight 255 was carrying 147 passengers, six cabin crew, and two Northwest pilots when it departed from Metro Runway 3-Center at 8:46 P.M. en route to Phoenix, Arizona.

There would be only one survivor.

Chapter 1

MOST DISEASES can be separated from one's self in the sense that it is possible to see them as a foreign, intrusive entity. Grief is not like that. Then again, perhaps it is. It is certainly intrusive. And to feel it in such intense, overpowering waves as I have experienced it is certainly foreign. But unlike other diseases one suffers over a long duration, I have found it impossible to separate myself from it. It is not as if there were this ailment—and also me. Over a period of time, the ailment has gradually *become* me, even as I have waited in vain for it to subside and finally end.

It does not end. It only changes form. Even as I begin to enjoy things again, even as I allow myself to believe that everything is nearly all right, I suddenly find my emotions coursing downhill, without brakes. Whatever is going on within me at such times makes no great amount of sense, but I am willing to make sense of it as soon as possible. As soon as I can understand things better. Or even at all.

I need to believe there are reasons for things. All things—great and small. It is part of my nature. It is the way I prefer to view the world. Certainly, there are events in life that cannot be explained as pure happenstance. They cannot simply be dismissed as freakish occurrences, as streaks of good or bad luck. They are too significant, too life-altering for that.

In order to meet someone with whom we intend to share our lives, an incredible combination of circumstances must somehow occur. The timing and precision involved in bringing two people together, over a distance that can span continents, is so unlikely that if it were only accidental, it would rarely, if ever, occur. The complex events that place us in the right place at the right time are so incomprehensible there is simply no way to explain it. And yet, it hints at something concrete and deliberate. *A specific plan.*

Something fated. It seems obvious to those who immediately share an uncanny sense of having known one another always, as though this were not their first meeting, but more of a reunion after many years of separation.

In September 1976, I was unexpectedly at the brink of such an experience. It lay just ahead as I attended a party that had been arranged for the winning sales team of a Phoenix real estate company I worked for. The party was being held in the home of one of the associates.

Although it was *my* team that had won the sales contest, I was not feeling particularly festive. I was a divorced mother of three. Having recently survived yet another failed relationship, I had slowly become resigned to an existence of aloneness. There was no longer anyone I wanted to share my life with, no one I wished to be married to.

As I moved out to the patio where the others were gathered, our host came up to me and introduced himself. "Hello," he said, "I'm Len Weite."

It was a moment in which I knew that something in this world knew me far better than I knew myself. I saw a man of medium height and stocky build, with blue-green eyes and a beautiful head of hair. As I looked at him, my sense of being hopelessly fragmented began to drift away. I no longer felt as if the pieces did not fit, but more as if they had suddenly, unexpectedly, found a true and proper alignment.

A while later, when Len asked me to dance, I found myself wondering why I was so attracted to him. After all, he did not in any way resemble my concept of the ideal man. He was not tall, not blonde, not stereotypically handsome, and yet, he *was* handsome and warm and charming.

After we danced, we sat and talked about his work—banking—and mine, about my family, my preferences in music, and a hundred other things. I very nearly forgot that I had come to this party with another man. By then, Len had also begun ignoring his guests. At the end of the evening, he gave me his business card, and I left on the arm of my disgruntled date.

That was the beginning of our relationship—Len's and mine. I did not know it at the time, for there was no reason to believe that anything could ever really come of us. *Us!* It shocked me to think that I had actually allowed such a word to enter my mind.

When Len called to ask me to lunch, I agreed but then had second thoughts and stood him up. The following day, I contacted him by phone.

"I don't suppose you'll really understand this," I said, "but I suddenly realized how wrong everything is. It may seem like an absurd position to take in the twentieth century but, the fact is, I don't go out with married men."

"I should have explained," came the soft and courteous reply. "My marriage is over and has been for a very long time. The fact is, I've moved out and am living with a friend."

"In that case," I told him, "I'll meet you anywhere."

We met at Treulich's Restaurant on Wednesday, September 15, 1976. And every year thereafter, we went there on that date.

The first time we met, we talked all afternoon, holding hands the entire time. We both knew that our feelings for one another were special. *That* was what we discussed most of the day. Later Len came home with me and I introduced him to my children.

When my girlfriend Sandy, who roomed with me, returned from vacation, she saw immediately that I had undergone some extraordinary transformation. I had the energy and enthusiasm of a teenager. I talked to her constantly about Len and started getting her out of bed at 6:00 A.M. to play tennis.

"Len's a very good tennis player," I hastily explained, "and so I've *got* to learn the game."

"Take lessons," Sandy suggested.

"I will," I said. "I'll do that too."

While I was happier than I had ever been before, I was also apprehensive. Looking back on my past history of relationships, I could not help feeling that I was somehow destined for disillusionment and pain. It did not help that Len was extremely loving and supportive. *When it finally stops,* I thought, *I'll just have that much farther to fall.*

We had only known one another for six weeks when Len proposed marriage. I remained cautious. Afraid.

"My divorce will be final in December," he told

me. "Can you think of a better way to start the New Year?"

The truth was, I could barely even think. I suddenly felt as though I were on a conveyor belt, being moved swiftly along, a little against my will perhaps, but certainly not against my heart. Reason. Logic. Practicality. I could no longer remember what those words had ever meant to me. I knew Len was what I wanted. It was as simple and as complex as that. In January 1977 we began to plan our wedding. We set the date for April 16. We were constantly together.

We traveled throughout Arizona, enjoying picnics and snowball fights. We had quiet dinners together and occasionally invited friends to join us. We spent time with my children and with his children. Late in the evenings, we would sit by the fireplace and dream.

There were the usual chaotic activities associated with planning a wedding and a 10-day Hawaiian honeymoon. By then, I had placed my home on the market. In the midst of all the confusion, realtors and potential buyers began to arrive. While it is difficult to keep a house in *showable* condition under the best of circumstances, these were clearly the worst. In one unforgettable instance, after Len and I had impulsively made love, we hastily made the bed and restored things to order only moments before the realtor arrived.

We took hundreds of photographs and sent one another endless cards. Often we separately sent each other the same card, with the same endearing message. It seemed to me that there was something truly uncanny in this, something incredibly magical, even miraculous, in all that we were discovering in ourselves and in one another.

By April 16, the date of our wedding, Len and I had both worn ourselves to a frazzle. That morning, as I prepared to leave to have my hair done, my youngest son, John, announced that the toilet in the guest bathroom was not working.

"It's got to work!" I told him. "There'll be fifty guests here for the reception. See if you can fix it! See if Len can fix it. Do something. Do something!"

A while later, I left the house in tears as Len and my boys huddled around the dismantled toilet, which the three of them had somehow managed to drag out into the backyard.

It was a prophetic sort of incident, in the sense that it seemed to set the course for the entire day. As my daughter and I drove to the church, we were nearly involved in an automobile accident. During the ceremony, one of my contact lenses fell out of my eye and lay unnoticed on my cheek until Len reached over and discreetly slipped it into his pocket.

Two hours into the wedding reception, I noticed Len looked ill. By the time we arrived at our suite at the Sheraton, he was vomiting and quickly became confined to the bathroom. He spent most of the night there, leaving me to watch reruns on television, which I did while sipping my lonely little glass of celebratory champagne.

It struck me as an ominous beginning for a marriage, if one chose to look at it in that light. Preferring to remain optimistic, I spoke excitedly about our Hawaiian honeymoon as my son drove us to the airport. Along the way, Len managed to spill a bottle of Pepto-Bismol all over himself. That was how our honeymoon began.

Our first-class flight included an enticing array of exotic food and drinks, which Len dared not touch out of fear of being confined to the cramped lavatory aboard the plane.

Fortunately by the time we arrived in Hawaii, he seemed a great deal better. We spent ten happy days in Honolulu and on the island of Maui.

In retrospect, our wedding day experiences gained in humor. We often reflected upon them as people are inclined to do once the more unpleasant and upsetting aspects of such events are safely behind them.

Returning from our honeymoon, we moved into a home we had purchased shortly before the wedding. Almost immediately, life became solid and pre-dictable. Each night, Len came home at precisely six o'clock. We would discuss the day's events, which, for me, consisted primarily of attending real estate school, where I was studying to acquire a broker's license.

In November, I opened my own office, and Len soon became an integral part of its operation. While I handled sales and managed the staff, he attended to the paperwork and accounting. After finishing at the bank, he would stop by my office. Afterwards we would go home together.

It was as pleasant and uncomplicated a life as any I could ever have imagined. It was exactly the way I had always dreamed a marriage might be.

One day, Len's ex-wife, Beverlee, came to my office and explained that she was moving to Las Vegas and did not intend to take their children with her. Len's son, Richard, was then twelve years old, and his daughter, Debra, only five.

I had originally met Beverlee through my work, since she was also in real estate. Now, rather suddenly, she was making a major change. I listened to her talk about her plans, not really understanding what she was trying to say until she had already gone. Leaving both children behind!

I was frantic at first, wondering how we would manage, since my son John and daughter Pamela were at home. There seemed no way to accommodate more.

Later that evening, Len and I decided that Richard would live with us and that Debra would live with Len's sister in New Jersey, where she would attend a

Catholic school with a little cousin who was exactly her age.

Once these arrangements had been made, we visited Debra whenever possible.

I was pleased to find that Len was an excellent father, very devoted to all his children and eager to spend as much time with them as he could.

Regarding his marriage to Beverlee, I knew it had not been a happy one, but he had wanted it to work. This was a quality I respected and admired in him.

My feelings for Len had grown much deeper, much more intense since our marriage. Unlike so many of my friends who spoke of becoming disillusioned with the everydayness of things, I continued to live in a state of constant expectancy.

Len made everything fun. I enjoyed fixing special meals for him and shopping for his clothes, since he was so appreciative of everything that was done for him.

We shared many special times together at our cabin in northern Arizona. We also took cruises with friends and visited Turkey and Israel. We toured the

Greek Islands and Rome, and visited Paris and London as part of a business trip of Len's.

Birthday celebrations were always special for Len. He looked forward to them with the expectancy and enthusiasm of a child. His own children adored him because he was such a good listener and problem-solver. He was also devoted to his mother and frequently arranged for her to visit us. He called her long distance every Sunday and traveled back East to see her as often as he could.

I particularly enjoyed our quiet times, our private times together. Each morning, Len prepared our morning coffee and brought it back to the bedroom. At this early hour, we would discuss our plans for the day and for the future.

Once we went to work, Len gave me little opportunity to feel separated from him. He often called me on his car phone just to tell me he loved me. Another endearing habit of his was to pick the roses off the bushes in our yard and to present them to me in a vase.

On my birthday, he would pile presents on our

bed and then sit watching me open them as we drank our morning coffee.

At Christmas time, he always selected the tree and then set up the antique trains his father had given him when he was very small. I was surprised to find that Len actually enjoyed shopping at this hectic time of year. He also enjoyed piling presents around the tree, lighting the fireplace, and making his own special eggnog.

On Christmas Eve, dinner usually consisted of homemade chili or clam chowder and cold cuts. After dark, we enjoyed driving around our neighborhood, admiring the lights and decorations on every street. Following Christmas church services, we returned home for eggnog and the opening of our gifts. Len was always the one who handed out the packages, reading aloud the names on every tag. Before very long, the living room was strewn with opened presents, paper, ribbons, and empty boxes.

On Christmas morning, I would always roast a turkey. Later in the day, friends usually joined us for dinner and drinks.

Each year, we celebrated the holidays in exactly

the same manner. It pleased me to think that we were doing things our own special way, creating our own traditions.

Len was extremely affectionate. Even after ten years of marriage, he continued to hold my hand in public, a habit of his our friends frequently commented on.

On those rare occasions when I was ill, it was a comfort just to have him around, for he was always smiling, always optimistic and cheerful.

As a depressed real estate market became more depressed, I no longer saw any valid reason to keep active in the residential market. With only commercial projects to concentrate on, I could now be home each evening when Len arrived. I saw at once how pleased he was to have me there.

Since I now also had more time to travel, Len and I began to spend weekends in San Diego on a boat with family and friends. After my son John had taken a job with a radio station in Portland, Oregon, we drove up the coast and visited him there. In 1985, Len and I visited Hong Kong. It was a trip that would continue to engender happy reminiscences for many years to come.

Once my daughter Pamela married and gave birth to a son, Christopher, Len and the boy became extremely close. The child constantly followed Len around, as did my oldest son's daughter, Stephanie, who responded to Len with the same kind of hero-worship.

By the time we started to make some long-range retirement plans, Len's son Richard was an engineering student at Arizona State University. His daughter Debra was enrolled at a private school in Scottsdale, Arizona, and was spending her weekends with us.

Family get-togethers were major events in our lives, with grown children, their spouses, and grandchildren coming to visit.

Following knee surgery, I hobbled around in an ugly cast and walked on crutches for a period of six months. Although I found this to be a totally frustrating experience, Len took it in stride and did all he could for me. Each night, he went through his ritual of "buttoning up the house." He checked the doors, windows, and thermostat, turned off the lights, then set a glass of water on the nightstand, and came to bed.

He was also the official family picture-taker. He once remarked that if anything ever happened to him, there would be no snapshots for me to remember him by, since he was always on the other end of the camera.

There are, of course, common devices to assist the memory—the log, the journal, the diary. Out of these sources, the following stand out:

—After the Christmas holidays of 1986, Len had to attend a business meeting in Florida. Afterwards we went on a 4-day cruise to the Bahamas. We then went to New Jersey for his high school reunion, an event he thoroughly enjoyed, seeing so many of his old classmates and friends.

—On our tenth wedding anniversary, Len decided it was time that I had a diamond wedding ring. After selecting the stone, we spent a great deal of time looking for just the right setting.

—On May 23, Len's 48th birthday, we invited

close friends and family to our newly redecorated home for a little celebration.

—On June 30, we went to San Diego, where we stayed in some lovely high-rise accommodations overlooking the beach. Len's comment on the last night of our stay was that this was the best vacation we had ever had.

—Our plans for August would have us going off in different directions for a while. I was going to visit my son Jim, who had recently moved to Memphis. Since Jim was in the process of setting up his new apartment, I thought I would be able to offer him some practical help. Len, meanwhile, was making plans to visit his mother in New Jersey. She was ill, and her birthday was due to be celebrated on August 16.

—Just before he left, we went to the jewelers and picked up my new ring. "You'll look like a queen wearing this," he said, as he slipped it on my finger. After ordering some custom shirts for Len at a tailoring establishment we regularly patronized, we walked to a nearby restaurant for lunch. That evening,

Debra and I prepared a special dinner for Len. I set the table with my best china and water goblets, thinking all the while how nice everything looked in our newly furnished dining room.

—On Thursday, August 13, 1987, Debra, Len and I drove to the airport. Debra had planned to visit a girlfriend in Las Vegas, Len was flying to New Jersey, and I was on my way to Memphis.

—After eating lunch together, Len walked Debra to the gate to catch her flight to Las Vegas. He and I then went on to the Northwest Airlines gate area to catch our respective flights. Kissing me goodbye, Len promised to call me as soon as he got in.

Once I'd arrived in Memphis, I spoke with Len several times on Thursday, Friday, and Saturday. On Sunday afternoon, I spoke with him again and he said he was anxious to get back home, to sleep in his own bed.

"As soon as Mom's birthday party's over with, I'm flying out of here," he said.

Since I had not planned on returning until the

following Tuesday, he said he would call me from home. We said our "good-byes," our "I love yous."

That Sunday evening, Len boarded a connecting Northwest Airlines flight to Phoenix. My thoughts had been with him all day. I could imagine his fatigue, his impatience, his eagerness to get home. It was no different with me. I wanted to be there, waiting for him, when he arrived. There was the sudden impulse to change everything around, to reschedule my own flight, to make some spur-of-the-moment arrangements. But then I told myself how foolish this was. There was no need. No hurry. It was only a matter of forty-eight hours.

Chapter 2

WHILE STANDING in front of the refrigerator in my son's apartment, I suddenly felt the pressure of a steel band around my head. After a moment it passed, but I mentioned it to my son. He suggested I lie down. I did so and gradually drifted off to sleep. Later, the sound of a telephone's ringing in Jim's room woke me up. Glancing at my watch, I saw that it was 9:00 P.M. Len would not be home until 10:30, so I knew it could not be him. Even so, I listened to the indiscernible drone of Jim's voice as he spoke in a low, quiet tone. Then, when he appeared in the doorway, I felt burdened with some heavy, sickening truth. I thought of the steel band around my forehead, the sharp pain, the incredible weight of it, like something relentlessly pressing me down. I counted the moments, the few brief moments that passed as Jim walked over to me. Taking my arm, he gently led me into his bedroom and over to the phone.

Something's happened, I thought, and later it will be important to have had these few moments of not actually knowing what it is.

I thought about my other children and my grandchildren. Somebody was sick. Or hurt. Or—I looked at Jim, knowing I should ask something. But what?

"Mom, Rich is on the phone. Len's plane went down."

I took the phone. I answered it. I heard Rich crying.

"What is it?" I asked. "Is Len hurt? Is he—dead?"

"Yes," he said, in a tone that made it unnecessary to clarify his answer.

It wasn't possible! I thought. I had spoken to Len only hours earlier—about his wish to get home, about the state of his mother's health, about her birthday, about his choice of a gift for her—a portable telephone that would make her life a little easier.

"It might be a mistake," I suggested to Jim. "Or he could have missed the flight."

Still grasping at straws, I walked to the television and quickly turned it on. I saw the news clip of the plane. I watched it explode into a fiery ball.

Afterwards, I felt myself moving through the apartment, pacing back and forth in a directionless frenzy. Inside, I could feel myself screaming—screaming and crying—but also, trying to sort things out.

I tried to pray. I talked to Len. I told him he was in my heart and mind forever. Even as I did so, I tried to picture how he might have been sitting, which way his face might have been turned. What had he known? How much had he sensed or suffered just before the end? The sudden pressure in my chest was like a dagger—like a shot. Final. Irreversible. *This was real!*

At 8:30 P.M., on August 16, 1987, Northwest Flight 255 was cleared at Detroit's Metro Airport. The captain and first officer discussed thunderstorms to be avoided on the way to Phoenix. After failing to make a required radio frequency change and taking a wrong turn on the taxiway, the plane rolled out on Runway 3-Center. At 8:42, the first officer advised the passengers that they were in number one position for departure and that they would soon be airborne.

Less than one second after take-off, Northwest 255 experienced the first sign of trouble. It began with a vibration in the pilot's control column. The jet climbed slowly, laboriously, rolling slightly to the right—then sharply, almost 30 degrees to the left. As the captain and first officer fought to control the bucking ship, a computerized voice in the cockpit warned of a stall. Fourteen seconds after take-off, when it should have been 600 feet in the air, the plane had only climbed 45 feet. Hurtling along at a speed of 222 mph, it clipped a light pole in a National Car Rental lot, shearing 18 feet off the plane's left wing. Witnesses reported that flames began to pour from the left engine, even as the plane struck another pole in the adjoining Avis lot. Then, as it fell into a 45° roll to the left, the plane scraped the Avis office's roof, did a half-cartwheel, and slammed into a concrete embankment.

Twenty feet of the 148-foot plane broke off and

skidded down a two-lane road, sliding under a railroad trestle and two spans of the I-94 freeway, leaving scattered fragments of metal and bodies in its wake. Pieces of the plane also killed two motorists on a nearby road. Total casualties on board: 155. Survivors: 1.

Moments before the crash—at 8:45 P.M.—a horrified air traffic controller, observing Northwest 255's erratic path, pressed the crash button on the tower console to alert other controllers. The alarm sounded in the airport fire station, and all incoming flights were flagged off. Within minutes, fire engines, ambulances, and police cars arrived at the site. The airport was closed down at 8:46. Passengers on other planes waiting to take off were told there would be a delay. Those already in the air were rerouted to Cleveland and other airports.

Seventeen area hospitals were notified to expect a heavy influx of injured. But as rescue workers searched among the scorched fragments of the plane, they found only bodies, or pieces of bodies. And then, one firefighter, alerted to the sound of a soft moan, discovered four-year-old Cecelia Cichan, the sole survivor of Northwest Flight 255; she was quickly rushed to a hospital.

Several hours later, there was still an unmistakable odor surrounding the crash site. Smoke from the cushions filled the air with the smell of burned plastic and wet wool. Dousing it with water had created a steamy vapor that now combined with the kerosene smell of residual jet fuel. The site, still smoldering from the post-crash fire, was checkered with yellow tarps that covered the bodies.

As the National Transportation Safety Board tried to assemble the more technical pieces of the puzzle, five pathologists, 11 investigators, and 20 dental forensic experts worked around the clock in an effort to identify the victims. It was determined that all had died from severe blunt force trauma. Rescue personnel recovered limbs, scalps, and torsos from the site. Pathologists working in a temporary morgue in a hangar attempted to match them up on the basis of size and clothing scraps. The condition of the bodies made visual identification nearly impossible, and also, gruesome. Only three were in a condition to be viewed by next of kin. The rest had to be identified through dental records, jewelry, watches, clothing, and shoes. By the following Saturday, six days after the crash, the last victim was finally identified and taken away in the last of the silver hearses.

The media version of the cause of the crash changed almost daily. There were reports that the plane had burst into flames at take-off, that it had suffered engine failure or wind shear. The FBI was brought in after rumors began circulating that there had been a bomb on board. This investigation was terminated when no evidence of an explosion could be found.

There were, however, significant clues still to be discovered, the first of which was the cockpit pedestal, which had housed the handle that adjusts a plane's flaps and slats. Extended on take-offs, the flaps and slats on the leading and trailing edges of the wings provide maximum lift, enabling the plane to rise rapidly. They also improve handling on take-off. Although setting the flaps and slats for take-off is part of the basic routine included in the required check-off procedure, the post-crash position of the flaps/slats handle on Northwest 255's cockpit pedestal was in a retracted position. This suggested that the jet's ability to climb quickly had been severely restricted.

Two other crucial items taken from the site were the Digital Flight Data Recorder and the Cockpit Voice Recorder, a 5" X 13" black box with an orange cover that preserved the crew's conversations and other cockpit sounds. The Digital Flight Data Recorder tape subsequently revealed that neither the slats nor flaps had been extended. Meanwhile, a member of the National Transportation Safety Board, in listening to the 32-minute black box tape, discovered that he could not hear the crew performing the routine taxi checklist. Assuming this had not been done, there remained the question of why there had been no computerized warning concerning the slats and flaps, as there should have been.

After five days of on-site investigation, the plane's most critical fragments were hauled to a Northwest hangar and shipped to labs and overhaul facilities around the country. The cleanup operation that followed uncovered a few more grisly reminders of the crash—a human shoulder bone and human scalp embedded with metal, broken eyeglasses, a flattened trumpet, charred snapshots, a single hard contact lens, and a burned watch with its hands fixed at 8:47.

Northwest 255 was, at the time of its crash, a six-year-old plane that had flown a total of 14,928 hours. Its last flight had been undertaken on a warm evening. There were scattered clouds in the sky and visibility of six miles. Although thunderstorms had been reported 20 miles north, a brief shower at the airport had already ended before take-off. And while several wind shear alerts had been announced that evening, there were none after 8:30 P.M. Overall, the weather did not appear to be a factor in the crash.

As time went on, more and more data pointed to a take-off with slats and flaps retracted, although they had been successfully extended by this flight captain and his first officer on six of the plane's previous take-offs and landings that day. A Northwest pilot who had hitched a ride on the Saginaw–Detroit segment of the flight two hours earlier recalled hearing the "flaps" warning when the crew made a sharp turn while landing at Detroit. And yet, this same warning device had not sounded on the plane's final flight.

As part of an investigation to determine the possibility of "pilot error," the backgrounds, training, and medical records of the crew members were closely examined. Autopsies revealed no traces of drugs or alcohol in either man's body or any evidence of disease. The only blemish on the first officer's record was a 1976 FAA fine for an unauthorized flight over a football field.

The pilot, on the other hand, had a flawless 32-year flight record, consisting of 20,859 flying hours. Although he was one of 1,000 Republic pilots obliged to take a pay cut after Republic's merger with Northwest, those who knew him well rejected the idea that this would have been enough to cause him to lose concentration or to become unduly negligent.

My own reaction to early investigative theories was that none of it really mattered and that nothing would ever matter again.

Returning home on an early morning American flight, I remember that a cabin attendant admired the necklace I was wearing. I told her that it had been an anniversary gift from my husband, and then burst into tears. I knew there would be no more happy anniversaries for me.

When we arrived at Sky Harbor Airport in Phoenix, my daughter, Pam, and grandson, Chris, were waiting. With them was Larry Goertzen, a co-worker of Len's. He was crying as he hugged me.

"Are you all right?" he asked.

"No," I told him. "Nothing will ever be right again."

For the next few days I lived on sedatives and juices to wash them down with. I wandered through the house, believing I could hear Len moving about in one of the other rooms. At day's end, I would find myself listening for his car in the drive.

I alternated between abject grief and raging anger. It did not seem to me that the edges of memory could ever be dulled—not about this. I felt certain that I would carry this dreadfully vivid scenario to my grave, remembering every ghastly nuance of it for as long as I lived. How long would that be? Probably not long, now that the desire to live had gone. I thought of going to sleep and not waking up again. Just slipping away—quietly, effortlessly. I found it a pleasant idea.

I would go back to Len, wherever that was, where *he* was, in soul or spirit. Why not? We belonged together. We were part of the same cloth. I had known the moment he died. Through that steel band around my forehead I had felt the impact of the crash.

"Don't suffer—don't suffer anymore," I found myself saying aloud. "Lie still. Don't struggle. Sleep in peace."

I wondered, had his face been calm or anguished at the moment of death? When his body was returned to us, would I dare—no, I would not dare. It would not be Len as I had known him, only some charred and mutilated remains. It sickened me to think that what came back to us might even be an inaccurate assortment of limbs, partly Len, partly someone else who closely resembled him in size or dress. Whatever it was would be the best that they had been able to do after sifting through the debris, and piecing together this gruesome jigsaw puzzle from human body parts that were twisted and torn, broken and burned beyond recognition. The best that could be done—to be accepted without question or complaint. *This was death*—as devastating as a curtain suddenly falling in the middle of a performance—too unexpectedly harsh and senseless—something no one could really be expected to understand.

That was it, I thought. *I do not understand this. There is no justice in it. No reason. No rhyme. I go to bed angry and wake up angrier the following day. The thought of death is gradually consuming me. It is like living on the edge of a huge dark pit. One false move, or possibly one deliberate one . . .*

As I tried to imagine how I would ever fashion a new life out of the shattered pieces of the old, the telephone rang constantly. It was to be expected, of course. But there were also *un*expected calls, including a sick call from a person who pretended to be an airline representative, who asked me how much I felt my husband's life was worth.

Each day there were more letters, more flowers and cards. First, a roomful and, finally, a houseful. People cared. They wanted to help, to show their affection and support. I was grateful in ways I could not properly express at the time, since my mind was constantly on Len—on getting him home.

My youngest son, John, came in from Denver.

Meanwhile, my older son, Jim, and Rich, Len's son, flew out to Detroit. While they were there, they were not asked to identify Len's body and were unsuccessful in locating any personal belongings.

For my own part, I continued to call Northwest, trying to learn something, trying to make some sense of things.

A memorial service was planned, and my sons and I selected a cemetery plot at a memorial park near our home.

Even as these things were being accomplished, I continued to deny Len's death. There was no body—and no goodbye—nothing but paperwork, ringing telephones, and general confusion. It might have been about anything—about anything at all.

Throughout our married life, Len and I had attended St. Paul's Catholic Church and that was where the memorial service was held. The church, that day, was filled to overflowing.

Afterwards, my family and I stood outside in the hot August sun and thanked everyone for coming. We then returned home with a number of close friends to a buffet that had been prepared by the St. Paul's Women's Club.

It was a long and exhausting day. That night, I fell into bed, prepared to be totally overpowered by my own fatigue, and yet, I could not sleep. I closed my eyes but the *images* remained, the fleeting pictures of the life I had shared with Len. How cold and lonely this world had suddenly become—so empty and silent and dark.

I was tortured by the realization that I did not know where Len's body was, that we should be held apart from one another in this last unexpectedly painful way.

When at last we received word from a local mortuary that Len's body had arrived, I became suddenly obsessed with the thought of establishing positive identification. The dental records I supplied for that purpose proved to be a match, but by then, I had already been told that Len was, in fact, "recognizable," although there were many broken bones.

When his wedding ring, which had apparently been included in the body bag, was returned to me, I suggested that it be placed on his finger. The mortician regretfully informed me that this would not be possible. At that devastating news, I asked that it be placed in the coffin along with his rosary, a religious medallion from childhood, and a picture of the two of us.

On Sunday, August 23, I went to the mortuary with Larry Goertzen and his wife, Ruth. As we stood silently together in front of the closed coffin, I found myself thinking of all the good times the four of us had shared. Now we had been brought together one last time by a horrible and senseless tragedy.

Len and Larry had enjoyed a long and amiable association, not only as personal friends, but also as co-workers at the bank where Len was Senior Vice President in Charge of Data Processing. When Northwest Airlines eventually called to say they had certain personal effects belonging to Len Weite, it would be Larry who claimed his wallet with its charred currency and partially melted credit cards. Several months would pass before I was finally ready to look at these items and accept their true significance. Early on, it seemed more important to keep myself distanced from such irrefutable evidence in an effort to somehow keep Len alive.

There were times when I still felt that he was with me, particularly when I detected a scent of after-shave lotion in the car or when I would suddenly discover a spare set of keys he had kept in some special place. At night, I would lie in bed and look up at the ceiling fan, momentarily intrigued by the pattern of plastic that surrounded it, which so closely resembled Len's profile. Whatever tricks my mind was playing on me provided a momentary buffer against reality, but reality was always there, waiting to intrude. It was in the sight of Len's old bathrobe hanging in the closet next to mine, it existed in my overwhelming grief, in the pain that often made me wonder how it was possible to hurt so much and still remain alive.

Len was gone, and yet I could see him and feel him everywhere. Something in my heart continued to insist that he was very, very close.

After we had attended the private service conducted by Father O'Carroll, the children and I discussed Len's death and the importance of remaining united and strong. We all agreed that we should continue to carry out family traditions, as Len would have wanted us to do. Even as we talked, I found myself wondering how it would be possible to do this. How could there ever again be a reason to celebrate major holidays, to plan summer vacations, to plan anything at all? I could not imagine myself doing these things with even a spark of enthusiasm or joy. Thinking about the long succession of days that lay ahead, I found myself wondering what I could possibly fill them with. It seemed to me that the abrasive quality of daily life, without someone to love and to share it all with, was a dismal existence at best.

In the weeks that followed, even as friends continued to write and to call, I tried to force myself back into some sort of normal routine. I often worked myself to the point of exhaustion, hoping to get a better night's sleep. How I hated waking up in the night with the sudden realization that Len was not there, and would not be coming back. I never turned down the covers on his side of the bed. And while I occasionally tried to think about the future, I knew that my life was in the past. Suddenly, I was someone to whom things had happened, not someone to whom things were happening *still*. I lived in a state of constant apprehension, fearing for the safety of other members of my family who might one day be lost to me as well.

What a cruel irony it was that I should be sitting alone in a newly redecorated home, feeling more like a stranger or trespasser now than someone who truly belonged. No, I no longer belonged here, I simply existed and might as easily have existed anywhere else.

I am not the person I used to be, I often found myself thinking. *I don't know who I am or where I am going. Sometimes I feel like the only person in the world. At other times, I feel invisible. Most of the time I feel dead.*

One day I spoke with Father O'Carroll, who referred me to a Grief Support Group. Although I attended several meetings, I found I could not talk about the accident, about my loss, in front of so many people. Private meetings with Sister Therese McIntyre proved more comforting but, somehow, did not eradicate the pain.

Eventually, I learned of the whereabouts of others who had lost loved ones on Flight 255. Once we had

49

met and talked, we formed a support group of our own. Meanwhile, life continued on.

It hadn't occurred to me that friends who were accustomed to thinking of me as Len's wife might treat me differently now that I was alone. Unfortunately, this more than occasionally turned out to be the case.

Because of my single status, I was sometimes looked upon as a threat to another woman's marriage. It hurt me, of course, to think that anyone would see me in this light, since my mind and heart were still with Len. I had no interest in cultivating a new relationship. The very thought was distasteful, even odious.

On impulse, I agreed to go to Hawaii with a couple with whom Len and I had vacationed several times before. When we arrived at our condo there, I began to move my things into the room we had always occupied. Suddenly, I heard the wife say: "You and your husband always took the best room. This time we'd like to have it."

While I was shocked by this, I offered no argument. On the one hand, I did not really care about the room arrangements. On the other hand, I was

offended by the need to discuss such an inconsequential matter so soon after Len's death.

I soon learned who my real friends were and,
without question, they were a generous number.
Invariably, these people sensed my need to talk about
Len, and frequently spoke of him themselves.

I am not certain what caused me to begin
documenting some of my thoughts and feelings.
Perhaps it was the need to find some form of
expression that I knew was totally private and safe.
Whatever I recorded on paper could not cause anyone
discomfort. I knew that no one could misunderstand
or judge me by those silent words, and so, the diaries
began:

> *How often I have heard a certain voice, a
> laugh—or seen a figure moving quickly
> through a crowd with that distinctive bearing
> and stride. I know it so well. I have it
> memorized. It hardly seems possible that it
> could be anyone else, and yet, it always is.*
>
> *I have made up my mind that you are*

gone, and that should make it easier. I only wish it would.

Obviously, my pain is not self-contained. I notice people's reactions to the expression in my eyes, to my speech, to my overall demeanor. What am I betraying in my efforts to appear composed? Something? Everything? Who can say? I have been trying not to care.

I would like it all to stop—those moments of automatic expectation. There is no longer any need to listen for your car in the drive, to anticipate a kiss and a hug as you come through the door. If only I could stop rushing home each evening, as if there were still some reason to be doing it.

You made me feel young and pretty and loved. Now, I feel a thousand years old. The image in the mirror is a strange one, so dismal and remote. I do not know that woman; perhaps I never will.

Tonight there is rain, and a room the color of midnight. By nature, I am compelled to work against isolation and loneliness in the only way I know how. Through you.

Talk to me.

Be with me.

Remember me always!

Death holds all the cards. It is the saddest sad and the loneliest alone.

We are condemned to be apart, unless God has yet another miracle in store. I wonder if He does? Another time? Another life? It is too much to hope for, and yet . . .

Chapter 3

—

Although information concerning Northwest 255 was still in the news, I found it difficult to absorb much of what was being said or written. It was as if I had developed a mental block on the subject. I would hear things and read things, but even as I tried to understand, the words would run together—as if they made no sense, or didn't really matter. It frightened me to think that I was losing my ability to comprehend or assimilate information. And yet, it seemed I had. But gradually, my powers of concentration grew stronger and, after a time, I even developed a morbid curiosity about things. Suddenly, it seemed important, even *necessary* to know!

What I was able to conclude from early news reports was that crash investigators had discovered conflicting physical evidence that prevented them from determining without laboratory tests whether the wing flaps of the plane were actually set in a take-off position. There were eyewitnesses who insisted that the flaps were indeed extended as the aircraft headed down the runway. Although the flaps did not appear to be extended at the crash site, investigators reasoned that they might well have retracted to a straight position upon impact.

Another theory involving the wing flaps was that the crew had, in fact, chosen correct flap settings, fooling the aircraft's electronic brain into thinking all was well, while the flaps themselves broke down mechanically and did not extend as they had been ordered.

There was also the possibility that the crew had failed to set the flaps and that the warning system broke down, preventing them from being warned in time to correct the omission.

Another factor to be considered was the weather. Fifteen minutes before the plane's departure, air traffic controllers had switched the direction of take-off, causing Flight 255 to lift off with a tail wind. Pilots generally prefer to take off and land into a head wind for the added safety it affords. When combined with the plane's full load and warm outside temperatures, it was suggested that the tail wind could have made it difficult for the plane to climb even with wing flaps properly extended. Thirty minutes before take-off, wind shears had been detected in the area; these sudden shifts in wind were occasionally strong enough to slam a plane to the ground.

Because a dozen witnesses insisted they saw the plane on fire, engine failure was another factor to be considered. Still, the data flight recorder indicated that the engines were producing adequate power. The plane's speed had certainly been normal for a take-off using flaps.

Finally, investigators planned to bench test the electronics pulled from the wreckage. In an effort to determine if electrical failure was involved, they would microscopically examine the panel warning lights.

The plane itself was a McDonnell Douglas model

MD-80 powered by Pratt & Whitney JT8D-217 jet engines. Each MD-80 wing is equipped with two sets of flaps—those on its leading edge, which are known as "slats," and those on its trailing edge, "tail-end flaps."

The MD-80, designed by McDonnell Douglas's commercial airframe division in Long Beach, California, is a fuel-efficient twin jet derivative of the DC-9 with an extremely good service record, unlike its DC-9 predecessor. According to a spokesperson for McDonnell Douglas, it functioned with 98 percent to 99 percent reliability, meaning that it had a good average for leaving the gate on time without mechanical delays.

In the case of Northwest 255, even though the plane was loaded to capacity with crew and passengers, it weighed an estimated 5,000 pounds less than its authorized maximum take-off weight of 149,500 pounds. It was a safe plane, carrying a safe load, and yet it had crashed.

Newspaper photographs of the rubble and wrecked vehicles along I-94, on Middle Belt Road, and in Avis's car rental lot, were grotesque and agonizing reminders of what had actually occurred.

When I finally requested it, I was sent a small chart showing the seating arrangement on the plane. Len's seat, 22A, had been toward the back, in the tail section. After the crash, Len's body had been found in that broken off section of the plane, lying beside a hill, near the underpass.

Almost immediately, there had been looters on the scene. Authorities arrested six of them as they sifted through the wreckage.

Aboard the plane were battered, scorched suitcases, a golf bag, a tennis racket, gift-wrapped packages, family photo albums, checkbooks, baseball cards, bent keys, wallets, charred money, melted credit cards, wallet-sized snapshots, and even a tiny baseball glove. Many family members were able to identify the bodies of loved ones through these personal possessions, even before a team of 20 dentists had painstakingly matched up dental records by x-raying victims' teeth and jaws.

Although it pained me to do so, I read about "shaken relatives grieving in seclusion." I read a firefighter's description of the scene—"there were legs, arms, hands everywhere. I stepped on one hand accidentally."

I read and reread detailed accounts of the plane's deadly course. The aircraft had skidded through three viaducts that were only two cars wide. At that point, there was no evidence of any wings.

An Oakland County sheriff's deputy, sent to assist Wayne County deputies, described the scene as worse than anything he had ever seen in Vietnam. There had been bits of bodies, tiny hands, people still strapped in their chairs trying to crawl away from the fire. Ultimately, there would be nine caskets filled with unidentifiable body parts.

In the continuing onslaught of articles—for that was how I eventually came to think of it—I reviewed arguments for and against airline deregulation. Apparently, lawmakers and consumer groups had begun to rethink the wisdom of deregulating this industry, in other words, giving it greater freedom in setting prices and schedules.

While it was the general consensus at the time that open competition was good for ticket buyers, there was also the feeling that the nation's air travel system was now becoming overburdened with too many flights carrying too many passengers.

Had it been overcrowded skies that resulted in a sudden runway shift for Northwest 255?

According to an August 28, 1987, *Detroit News* report, a last-minute runway switch had forced the pilot and co-pilot of Northwest 255 to refigure wing flap settings and other crucial take-off conditions previously calculated by the airline's computer. This recalculation, according to investigators, while not a rare occurrence, was one of several interruptions the crew had been subjected to as it prepared to take off, and may have contributed to the confusion in the cockpit before the crash.

Normally, minutes before departure, flight crews are provided with computer printouts that contain suggested take-off speed and flap settings. Such calculations are based on the plane's weight, its center of gravity, its runway assignment, and the direction of take-off.

The calculations on Flight 255's printout were based on the assumption that the pilot would take off into the southwest on a 10,500-foot runway called 21-Right. But as the plane began to taxi, air traffic controllers at Metro airport switched the flight to Runway 3-Center, an 8,500-foot runway that would head the plane in a northeasterly direction. Forced to scrap their original computer analysis, the captain and co-pilot had to refigure flap settings and critical take-off speeds in the cockpit, using on-board charts and equipment. This task was further complicated by a slight tail wind, which made take-off more difficult and required a longer runway roll, even though they were now on a runway that was 2,000 feet shorter. During their taxi, as the pilots continued with their checklist and attempted to refigure take-off speed and flap settings, they missed a taxiway and were directed to turn around. The tower also interrupted twice with weather updates. The cockpit voice recorder later showed that the pilots made no verbal confirmation of flap settings before take-off. Although Patrick Broderick, the president of Air Safety International in Atlanta, declined to speculate on how the recalculation might have affected the crash, he admitted there was a possibility that it could have been a factor.

So many theories, opinions, and ideas to be considered. While they were all being voiced by so-called "reliable sources," they did not always coincide with eyewitness accounts. I read it all, and thought and thought about it until my head was spinning.

And then suddenly, there was the ugly legal ordeal to be faced. Soon after the crash, San Francisco lawyer Melvin Belli filed a suit in U.S. District Court in Phoenix, Arizona, on behalf of a woman whose young son had been killed in the crash. Two other lawsuits had been filed earlier in the same week, and more than a dozen had already been filed on a national basis.

Insurance underwriters estimated that the crash of Northwest 255 would cost aviation about $200 million in losses for the craft and in passenger liability claims.

Although I had known that a lawsuit was inevitable, I had not given any great amount of thought to the manner in which the value of a human life would actually be calculated. In all truth, it seemed like an impossible thing to do. Yet, only hours after the crash, attorneys and insurance underwriters were already working on the economics of this tragedy. In the final analysis, it was all pretty cut and dried.

Insurance settlements were lower for children who died than for those who were injured and survived. Settlements on deceased doctors, lawyers, engineers, professors, and truck drivers were figured by income formulas and actuarial tables. A housewife was valued at whatever her domestic services would bring in the marketplace of the community in which she resided.

Settlement offers from Northwest's insurance underwriters could be rejected, of course, but if a family chose to sue, it might have to wait several years for the case to be heard. And then, relatives would once again be forced to relive the tragedy in the course of giving testimony.

Weighing the somber reality of this, I knew I could not possibly survive several years of litigation. Simply surviving was enough in itself.

Although I had imagined that engaging the services of an attorney was a course of action I would need to initiate, I soon found myself being approached by attorneys who were extremely eager to take my case. Without exception, they all insisted that I needed immediate representation, that there was no other way of protecting my own interests. Unable to cope with the pressure that was constantly being exerted upon me, I turned to my son, John, who contacted Houston attorney Joseph Jamail. After a personal consultation, it was mutually decided that Mr. Jamail should represent me. I did not immediately realize who this man was, that he had successfully represented Pennzoil in their suit against Texaco. For the moment, I was more preoccupied with his discomforting prediction that my suit would probably take a couple of years to settle.

A couple of years! I found myself wondering what I would do in the interim. It seemed to me that nothing could really be decided about the future until I had successfully resolved the past, although, for me, resolving the past had little enough to do with a financial settlement. With Len's death, money was all that could be paid. There was no other way in which to be compensated for this incredible loss. But that was less important than to finally have it over with. For quite a while now, I had been living for a day when some significant thing would finally happen that would relegate all of this ugliness to the past. On such a day, it seemed to me that I would wake up and suddenly find myself whole again. Perhaps settling the lawsuit was the manner in which to accomplish this. I hoped it would be. I *wanted* it to be!

I was beginning to feel the isolation that comes when others start drifting away. I knew they were uncomfortable with the person I had become, a person whose grief was still too visible. How odd that was, since I was making a deliberate effort to appear calm and composed. But perhaps that was it. They did not see the calmness and composure. Only the effort involved.

As for me, I was certainly conscious of the effort; at times, it literally exhausted me. At home, alone, I would give in to fits of frustration, to crying jags, and to periodic moods of depression.

I sat and sorted through the items of Len's I felt it had been important to keep. An old cotton robe. A pair of leather work gloves. Some cowboy boots. A headband and wristband he had worn while playing racquetball. An old pair of socks. Some loud Hawaiian

shorts. A broken wristwatch. Such an odd con-
glomeration of things. For a time, I wore the robe, but
only until it began to lose Len's scent and began
acquiring mine.

There was also a briefcase with a 4-16 combination—the date of our anniversary. A class ring. A
baby picture of Len, and some old cleaning cloths he
had used to wash the car. A totally senseless and
absurd collection of items. As senseless and absurd as
the thing that had taken him away.

It frightened me to suddenly lose control, to find
myself crying as I made a bed, straightened a closet, or
brought in the morning newspaper. Although I was
not always conscious of thinking about Len, he
remained a constant presence in my life.

Fearing that I might be losing touch with reality, I
became determined to learn what I could do about the
various stages of grief. Through private counseling
sessions and through printed material on the grieving
process, I discovered that the stages tend to follow a
specific pattern:

Shock—In this initial stage, a person is virtually
anesthetized against his or her loss and may be unable

to comprehend or face the magnitude of what has actually occurred.

Emotional Release—In this second stage, there is an emotional reaction to loss that should never be suppressed. Those who do not permit themselves to become angry, or to cry, greatly impede their overall ability to recover, and often suffer delayed reactions, possibly months or even years later.

Depression—In this stage, it is usual to experience the pervasive feeling that everything is hopeless, that nothing or no one can help. While it is altogether normal to experience such depths of despair, whenever possible, these feelings should be openly expressed to someone who can assist the sufferer in placing them in the proper perspective.

Physical Symptoms of Distress—In situations where a loved one has died after an extended illness, the survivor often suffers some of the same symptoms as the victim.

Panic—Convinced that "something is wrong with me," a survivor may suddenly find it impossible to concentrate on anything else. There is the fear of losing one's mind, or at the very least, of behaving in an abnormal or conspicuous manner.

Guilt—At this stage, the survivor may begin to berate himself for behaving in a cruel or neglectful manner toward the lost loved one. Such behavior is often imaginary or highly exaggerated, although it may occasionally have some basis in fact. Whatever the reason for guilt feelings, it is important to learn to live beyond them and to forgive oneself.

Hostility—As the survivor begins to "feel better," various forms of expression may become more active. Hostility toward those who are felt to be "to blame" is altogether common but should not be perpetuated over long periods of time.

Inability To Renew Normal Activities—In this stage of grief, the survivor finds it difficult, if not impossible, to return to a normal routine, for instance, get back to business as usual. By now, the survivor is becoming resigned to bearing the loss alone as others turn their attention back to their own activities. At this juncture, it is important to avoid them at all costs.

Gradual Overcoming of Grief—As an emotional balance slowly returns, the healing process continues.

The actual rate of healing will, of course, vary from one individual to the next.

Readjustment to New Realities—In this final stage, the survivor must face some irrefutable facts. Life will never be the same. The old self is gone, but through healthy bereavement, one can often become a stronger, deeper person—and certainly one more sensitive to others in a similar situation.

In reviewing these various phases, it seemed to me that I was constantly vacillating between stages seven (Hostility) and eight (Inability to Renew Normal Activities), almost as though I were stuck there. Whenever I expressed concern over this, my counselor told me not to worry, that everything was normal. I hardly saw how this was possible. Having moved so far away from the person I once was, I could not imagine how anything about me could ever be normal again. I lived alone in a silent house that had once been filled with activity and laughter. I brewed my own coffee now, not nearly so well as Len had done it—or perhaps it was our morning conversations that gave it that added flavor. Now, there was no one to discuss my day with, no one to make plans around, no one to lean on in that very special way. Len had understood me better than anyone else in the world. He had known, instinctively, what it took to make me feel happy and secure. How did I feel now? Fragile. Uncertain. Hopelessly fragmented. I could not bear the thought of ending my days without Len. A day at a time, I was constantly being told. Take it a day at a time.

All right then, today I will live without him and not think about forever. I will not think about having no one beside me, about having so many questions and so few answers. I will perform my little ritual of daily tasks, which now include all the things that Len once attended to. Monthly bills still need to be paid. Whatever breaks still needs to be fixed. I am inclined to include myself among the things that need to be fixed, but for that, there is no handyman to call.

A new relationship is impossible—at least for the present. Even in purely social situations, I find myself making immediate comparisons. The way a man moves and talks and speaks with me. Pleasantly, politely enough—but not as Len would have done it. It is all so ridiculous and unfair. There is automatic conflict, because we cannot communicate, because there is nothing to be said. My concept of reality is so different from that of another. We could debate the issue forever—how things should be, and *need* to be, and *are*—but what would be the point of it all? I wanted things as they were. The thought of a "new life" was frightening. I knew what I had, but I didn't know what I might get.

Outwardly, I must often have appeared to be bad-tempered, censorious, or snobbish. It saddens me to think so, since people were basically kind to me. They wanted to cheer me, to please me, to make me feel better about things. I understood their need to do this, for I was a constant reminder of what could happen to us all. I would have liked to suggest something else in people's minds, in my *own* mind, if only there were a way to do so.

I wish I could re-involve myself in things that Len and I enjoyed together. Brunches. Movies. Weekend shopping trips. Nowadays, I go to church, and then I visit the cemetery. I sit by Len's grave and talk to him as I always did, and for the same reason. I am still in need of his love and understanding.

Len—I wish I could see this day as you and I would have seen it together. I'm sure it must be a really lovely day for those who are able to perceive it in that light. There are flowers, and birds, and billowy clouds, and a gentle breeze that softly stirs the leaves. I still notice these things, if some deliberate effort is made, but the scene is altogether different now—so flat and one dimensional, as if all the color had been drained away.

I cannot speak of my feelings to anyone, for people expect me to be "better" now. Each time we meet, I feel I am being measured in terms of the progress I've made—as if I were on a conveyor belt, moving straight ahead, out of my period of mourning into some new and brilliant light. A light of higher wisdom and understanding. I have even had people speak to me in these terms, as if they were offering the promise of some compensatory prize for all that has been lost. In the end, I am expected to garner something positive from all this, and to actually be grateful for it. They do not know. There is nothing to be garnered except emptiness and sorrow. And a persistent curiosity about the remainder of our life together. How it would have been. How well we would have aged together. I believe we would have exhibited a rare talent for that, knowing how to complement one another's frailties, as mind and body gradually failed. I have seen this done well. And I have also seen it done badly,so that only anger, resentment, and bitterness remained. I cannot imagine us that way, not together—but that is how I am alone.

Because I was not with you on that plane, I am thought to be a survivor. And yet I did not survive the crash of Flight 255. The life I knew and cherished died when you did. The person I am now is a stranger, even to me. I am not better and stronger for what I have faced. It has left me feeling frightened and insecure. The need for support and caring continue.

I am so lonely without you. I pray, I write, I look after the house and car. I listen to the news, I shop and contact friends. Much of the time I travel, which enables me to be lonely in strange places.

In church today, I kept thinking of the empty seat beside me. I do not remember the service. I remember only how you used to hold my hand.

Len, I am not handling this well, but I cannot bear to have you think I do not try. I do try. I am trying! Show me how to do it better, and I promise you, I will.

Sleep well, my love.

Chapter 4

━━━━━

WHENEVER it was necessary to change or to replace anything in the house, I would find myself thinking: *This was here when Len was here.* Discarding the item meant letting go of yet another little piece of our life together. It had to be done slowly, in stages, in order to be done at all.

The house itself was quiet, so quiet that I could hear my own breathing. Once it had been filled with life. So many happy and exciting things had occurred here, a constant stream of activity that seemed to have no end. But now all that had ended. The house had died with Len. Looking about, I tried to think of a way in which to revive it, to make it bright and cheerful again. But this was nothing that paint or wallpaper could cure. And anyway, everything had already been done. So recently remodeled, it was now a house that *others* admired. To me, it was as cold and lonely as a tomb. The house and I both seemed to be waiting, as the hours continued to tick by.

Hours.

Days.

Weeks.

I did not think about them or plan them but simply allowed them to flow.

How would Len have done it? I wondered. How would he have managed his grief? Management and organization were *his* talents, not mine. He was more of a realist. He was also more people-oriented. Throughout my life, it had always taken me a very long time to form relationships, which perhaps accounted for my inability to let go. Even after something was over, it was not yet over for me. How else could I explain the fact that I could still cry over the loss of my parents, who had both died when I was a child?

I was too private a person, too emotionally

reclusive. It was extremely hard for me to show or express my feelings. I was hesitant to betray too much of myself, fearing vulnerability.

At night, I lay in bed and thought about who I was and who I was gradually becoming. At times, it seemed as if there were no longer a person there, only this inner weakness, this uneasy sleep, this nagging pressure of something that needed to be done.

Now and again, a wonderful memory would filter through, one that would bring back every word, look and gesture to be associated with a happier time. Suddenly. Unexpectedly. And then, just as suddenly and unexpectedly, it would be gone.

I still had Len's voice on the tape of our answering machine. Occasionally, I played it, wanting so much to bring him close, to have his voice back in the house again.

One night he appeared to me in a dream, which gradually developed into a series of dreams in the sense that they all seemed to be woven from a common thread. In each case, I found myself surrounded by people who seemed to know where Len had gone and why he had abandoned me. When I asked them to explain it, they would immediately move away. Enraged by this obvious conspiracy, I determined to uncover the truth. But while the dreams continued, the answer never came. And then, one night, the dream took an entirely different turn. This time, I stood in a hospital corridor, trying in vain to get into a room where nurses surrounded Len's bed. Because I was not permitted to enter, I somehow arranged for my son John to smuggle him out of the room. John carried Len home in his arms and placed him in our bed. That night, I held Len close, but all he would say to me was that he wanted to die. And then, suddenly he was back in the hospital, and I was back out in the hall. As I looked into his face, I heard a nurse say, "He's gone." Turning to Richard, I said, "You'll have to take your father's company car back to the bank," and that was the end of the dream. This dream differed from all the others in that it actually dealt with Len's death, which I no longer seemed to be denying.

Was this progress of a sort? It was difficult to say.

There was only one more dream. In it I felt Len's presence in the room and his lips pressed against mine. When I awoke, I bolted upright in bed, for I was still conscious of his warmth and the ticklish feeling of his moustache against my skin.

After that, there were no more dreams. It was as though he had returned to me one last time, if only to say goodbye.

Goodbye. It was an impossible word to say or to accept in circumstances such as these. There had been no time for goodbyes. We had not been granted that moment, a moment that might have helped to make things easier to bear.

The crash itself was all the more tragic because of the way in which it had so quickly been relegated to the past. One hundred and nine people from Phoenix and outlying areas had perished on that flight, but no great amount of attention was ever given to this. The more I thought about it, the more I believed some recognition should be paid. After all, our own state had suffered the greatest losses. Why weren't we doing something in commemoration?

City and state officials with whom I discussed the matter seemed to feel that a permanent memorial was certainly in order. I was urged to keep everyone advised of my progress. At an appropriate time, it was felt that some donations could undoubtedly be raised, although no one actually volunteered to take on the task.

In the end, our local support group of Northwest 255 survivors decided to sponsor a 1950's theme dance that would be open to any media people who might care to attend. Although I had imagined that any number of local hotels would be willing to provide accommodations gratis for such an event, none offered to do so. The dance itself was never held.

At that time, our local support group consisted of approximately 30 members. Robin Spotleson, whom I met at the first meeting, became a lasting friend and later helped to arrange the private memorial service that was held on August 16, 1988, the first anniversary of the crash.

Robin, who was in her early 30s, had lost her only child, 12-year-old Justin, on Flight 255. The boy was returning home after visiting his grandparents. It was an exciting experience for Justin, the first time he had ever been permitted to travel alone. He was an extremely religious boy and was carrying his Bible at the time of the crash. Despite looters' attempts to steal the Bible, it was returned intact after it was recognized among certain personal effects.

Over a period of time, as Robin and I became better acquainted, we also learned to turn to one another, particularly on certain dates when we knew the other would be having a hard time. After Robin had visited my home and my family, I visited with her and met her husband.

From Northwest's chart of the actual seating arrangement on Flight 255, I determined that the seat next to Len had been occupied by Louis Scarseletta of Lockport, New York. On impulse, I wrote to his wife Kathy and invited her to correspond with me. She did so, enclosing a picture of herself and their three children. From her letter I learned that her husband had been 30 years old at the time of his death, and that he, like Len, was involved with computers.

My association with Robin and Kathy did much to reinforce my feelings about a memorial service. When it was finally held, it was all that I had hoped it might be.

Following an invocation by the pastor of Valley Cathedral Church, the name of each victim was read.

This was followed by a musical interlude. After the reading of a scripture by a Jewish Rabbi, Robin and I each gave readings of our own. This was followed by comments from a Catholic priest, another musical interlude, and finally, a closing prayer.

The 500 or so who were there seemed deeply moved by the service, even as I was.

Once it was over, I fully expected to experience a kind of *finality* about things. For a very long while, I had been looking for a way to bring an end to my grieving, to somehow relegate it to the past in order that I might contemplate a future. Without realizing it, I had been working toward an official "cut-off point", a point at which I could say: "I have finally come through this and now I am whole again." I thought the memorial service would be that closure/start-up point.

But nothing was different, and suddenly it occurred to me that this might always be the case. The second year might be no better than the first, nor even the third or the fourth.

In June I had gone to the Idyllwild School of Music and Arts, a quiet place outside Palm Springs,

where I participated in a creative writing course. I met
some wonderful people there, including the instruc-
tor, Norman Corwin. He had urged me to write
spontaneously, on any subject that interested me. I had
written about Len, and the tragedy that had taken him
away:

> *I cannot say that suffering has made me a*
> *better person. I feel bitter, angry, and sad. The*
> *pain is still with me. My life is on hold.*
> *Nothing is settled with the airline. My health*
> *has suffered because of this stress. I do find*
> *comfort in my writing and sincerely hope that*
> *it will help someone, someone who is presently*
> *experiencing grief and the underlying fear that*
> *they are going mad.*
>
> *The fact is, it is difficult to function well*
> *once your family security has been destroyed. It*
> *is also difficult to do things alone that you have*
> *always done with someone else.*
>
> *Recently, I went to a small Italian*
> *restaurant for dinner. I felt so strange sitting at*

a table alone with an empty chair beside me. Everywhere I looked, I saw couples enjoying their meals and one another's companionship. Finally, I asked the waitress to box up my dinner so that I could take it home.

What can God possibly have in store for me? Why was I spared? When will everything fall into place and begin to make some sense again?

I feel that loneliness hurts—it is a detriment. I need some validation that I am still alive.

Pain is a difficult thing to describe.

Whenever I think of Len, I feel a sudden rush of love—an inner warmth. I have stored up enough memories of our time together to last as long I last. They say that life comes full circle. If it does, I want to be with Len again.

Whenever I hear that another airliner has

crashed, I see it as yet another heart-shattering, life-shattering tragedy. A tragedy caused by man, not God. Horrifyingly senseless, a tragic waste of precious lives, a product of indifference or careless disregard for basic safety procedures.

Suffering of this kind should make everyone stop and think, and encourage them to take increased precautions. Tragedy should not be without meaning. There is no blessing to be found in suffering. People are shattered and ruined by suffering rather than helped by it. Suffering embitters those who survive. Yes, I am bitter. Bitter, helpless, and sad. I have not yet been able to work through this grief. I cannot accept this senseless loss.

I cannot grieve openly, for that is too discomforting to others. I must go off by myself, feeling isolated and alone whenever I do.

I feel that friends should help to keep the memory of lost loved ones alive. They should *allow themselves to talk about them, to remember, and grieve. My Len is worth grieving about. Life is not fair. The wrong people die too soon.*

I know I must find my own path to peace, but where do I get the strength to go on? Once you have reached a certain age, you are expected to enjoy a certain quality of life, some measure of security, the love of children. And, of course, it is envisioned that you will "grow old gracefully" with this one special love of your life.

Everything was there in the beginning, but now it is gone. I wish there was some magic medicine that could fix this, this chronic internal distress. I sometimes feel panic because I cannot seem to think of anything except my loss. Len was so terribly important to me, and suddenly, he was taken away. I suffer daily, whenever it occurs to me that he is really gone forever. It makes me want to run away from life, to avoid attaching myself to anything new.

Since everything has changed, I wish that I too could change. But this is not an easy thing to do. Dreams die hard for me.

This is a very personal writing, without benefit of any structure or polish. It says what I feel for now. I do not know about the future.

Perhaps it will be possible to find some new meaning in life, some person to care for and someone who cares for me. I must try to remain open to that idea. If I only knew what to do, where to go, and how to begin!

I was surprised to discover that whenever my work was read aloud, it caused emotional reactions in others. Although the writing itself was frequently complimented, I was more inclined to believe that people could identify with what I was saying because of experiences they themselves had had. Looking into their faces, I was tempted to ask how they had managed to come through or in what way they were still in it.

Pain, insofar as I was able to perceive it, is a feeling that repels, just as pleasure attracts. Those still experiencing pain are generally concerned with the thought of bringing it to an end. If we are sick, we consult a doctor. If we are cold, we look for warmth. If we have suffered a loss—what do we do? Anything material can be replaced with something else of a material nature. But the loss of a loved one is quite another thing.

To somehow live *past* it seemed to be the only answer. Obviously, I had not yet managed to do this, perhaps because of circumstances and events that constantly brought Len back into my life. My suit against the airlines. The daily responsibilities that had once been his concern instead of mine. How long would it be before the life I was living was totally my own, not one constantly associated with Len? Would everything change if I were to move somewhere else, to adopt another lifestyle, to surround myself with an entirely new group of friends? Whose life would it be then? No, it seemed to me that I needed to continue on with the person I was, living as that person would live, surrounded by old and familiar friends. There was nothing to be gained from escaping into other worlds or other identities. I simply had to come to terms with life as it was.

Survival depends on the right answers. If a person is lost in a forest, his survival depends on taking the right path. By the same token, each day there are new choices to be made—hopefully, the right ones, the kind that bring pleasure instead of pain.

Pleasure was not a word I had given any great amount of thought to. Not in a very long time. What had I thought about? Such words as *coping* and *enduring* immediately came to mind. While these were certainly poor substitutes for happiness or pleasure, I recognized them as part of the process, part of what I needed to experience in order to get from one plateau to the next.

My major concern was that I might not be moving in any direction at all. In reviewing the various stages of grief, I could see where I had already moved through several of them. Still, there was no denying that I frequently fell back into an earlier stage rather than advancing to the next. At times, it seemed that I existed in several categories at once. I was both angered and frustrated by this, since I wanted to do more for myself but had no real idea as to what it was I should do.

Among other things, Len's death had made me realize that I had never really considered the possibility that the clock might be running out for us. While I had known theoretically this must eventually happen, I had always envisioned it at some "far-off time," when we would both be very old. Then, too, I had always assumed that *I* would die first, perhaps because I believed it more *convenient* to die first. Whoever died would automatically be spared the ongoing agony of loneliness and grief, the very agony I was experiencing now.

At this point, the overriding fear was: *What if I can't stand on my own?* I knew I could survive financially and that I had certain professional skills to fall back on. I could occupy my days by traveling, or working, or by visiting with friends and family. I could keep busy and carry on as if nothing had really changed. I could do this so convincingly that, in time, others would begin to admire my ability to bounce back. I could even appear to support the theory that Time was a Healer, although I knew it was only an Insulator. Once enough time had passed, I would be adequately distanced from this horrible tragedy, so that every aspect of it would not immediately rush to mind at the slightest provocation. There would be all those other new things that had happened in between. Memories of the past with Len would first need to work themselves through all the new events in my life before they could actually be re-experienced, and thus they would gradually become weaker or vaguer in my mind.

One of the most dramatic changes in my life concerned itself with the fact that where light had once been, now I sensed only darkness ahead. It seemed to me that my suit against Northwest Airlines would never be settled. I had never imagined that there could be so many postponements and often suspected that these were being deliberately contrived in order to get me to drop the case.

As the time for my deposition drew near, I was advised of what would occur and what I should prepare myself for. Yes, it would be hard. The questions would be probing and concern themselves with matters I would rather not discuss. I would need to answer as honestly and as thoroughly as I could. I was urged to take my time in order to avoid becoming flustered.

Here was something *else* to be dreaded, a line of intensive questioning aimed solely at diminishing my marriage and the value of the life that had once been Len's. Whatever else happened, I vowed to stand my ground. If nothing else were accomplished, I would somehow manage to convey what I felt about what had been lost. I would see that everyone heard and clearly understood. This was no small, inconsequential matter. It concerned itself with suffering and death, and with living out the grim reality that must inevitably follow.

Chapter 5

_____

ON JUNE 30, 1989, I appeared at the offices of a local Phoenix law firm to give a deposition related to my case against Northwest Airlines.

At 12:05 P.M., Northwest's attorney, H. William Fox, began his questioning. I was asked to give my name, age, place of residence, and marital status. As concerned my personal background, I testified that I had been born in southern Illinois, and had attended high school in Johnston City, Illinois.

Soon after high school graduation, I married my first husband. My three children, James, Pamela and John, had all been born from that marriage, which later ended in divorce.

I moved to Phoenix in 1963 and worked as a legal secretary. Finding that this provided an inadequate income on which to raise three children, I realized that I did not really need a job. What I needed was a profession.

After obtaining a real estate license, I joined the staff of an office that was affiliated with Century 21, a franchised real estate firm, where I worked in residential sales. During the first quarter of 1977, I obtained my broker's license and also married Len.

During this particular phase of testimony, I was asked to clarify the manner in which the two of us had first met and the situation that existed at that time between him and his estranged wife.

"Before the separation, did you discuss with him at all his plans to separate?" William Fox asked.

"No."

"Is it your belief or impression that you were in any way involved—the meeting with you a week before was in any way a motivating cause of the separation?"

"Absolutely not."

"After your first meeting at the party and after his

separation, how did you next make contact with Mr. Weite? Did he call or . . ."

"He called me."

"And did you then begin dating?"

"We did, after I ascertained that he was indeed separated and the marriage was over . . ."

"You ascertained that by asking him?"

"Yes, I did."

In the questions that followed, I was asked about Len's two children, particularly about their emotional state at the time of their parents' separation and pending divorce. I described Len as an excellent and devoted father, and the children as altogether typical for their ages, with no visible abnormalities.

When asked to explain the manner in which Len's children had come to live with us, I responded by saying that their mother had come to my office one day to tell me that she was moving to Las Vegas, that she intended to change her lifestyle, and that she needed to leave the children behind.

At the time of the deposition, Len's son, Richard, was an aerospace engineering graduate of Arizona State University. My own daughter, Pamela, had married and divorced, and she and her son, Christopher, were living with me. My son, John, at that time was working as a disc jockey in Sacramento.

Early questions about Len's daughter, Debra, concerned themselves with the manner in which she had come to live with her Aunt Eileen and how well she had adapted to this.

I explained that Len frequently visited his daughter, that he had obtained legal custody of his children by court order, and that his ex-wife had moved to Las Vegas.

When she was eight, Debra had returned to Phoenix to live with Len and me, and attended public school for approximately two years. At the end of that period, she lived with her mother for a time and then returned to us. Noticing some disciplinary problems, we had enrolled her in a private school.

"Did she speak out against you?" William Fox was curious to know.

"No, not really," I said. "Her father wouldn't allow that."

"Did she speak out against him?"

"No, she loved her father very much."

When asked how she and her brother had gotten along, I admitted that they sometimes squabbled as siblings were known to do. Overall, I considered Debra exceptionally bright, which was certainly substantiated by her scholastic record whenever she seriously applied herself.

The next series of questions concerned themselves with our summer vacations, which were generally spent in the San Diego and Mission Beach area. I explained that we had a 36-foot trawler moored in Harbor Island that we used on a time-share basis. When asked if the children ever accompanied us, I said that they did, that these were essentially "family vacations."

Questions concerning Len's death were not introduced until the deposition was nearly three-fourths completed.

"What was the occasion for Leonard's trip to the East?" William Fox finally asked.

"Leonard's mother had been very ill," I said. "We had been back there about three months prior and had gone to visit her in the hospital. The priest had come and said last rites, and we went back there fully expecting to go to a funeral, and she rallied somewhat and then seemed to get—she got well enough to go home to his sister's house. And . . ."

"Is that to Eileen's house?"

"Yes. And her Mom's birthday was August 16th and . . ."

"He went to see her?"

"Yes."

"Did you and Leonard ever have arguments?"

"We were married. Yes."

Following some off-the-record discussion between William Fox and my own attorney, Joseph Jamail, Fox's questions continued.

"Did you ever have any serious arguments with him? And by serious, I mean something that caused either him or you to threaten divorce or threaten separation?"

"No, never. Never. Leonard and I were—when Leonard went back to see his mother, that was one of the few times that we were apart. And we tried to plan it so we'd be apart the least number of days. I went to help my son and he went to see his mother."

It occurred to me suddenly that these questions

were specifically designed to establish the "monetary worth" of the marriage, which was apparently determined, at least in part, by how well the parties did or did not get along.

After a brief recess, the questioning resumed, and once Len's will, our tax returns, and other financial information had been discussed, Fox once again returned to the subject of Len's children. Suddenly, almost as an afterthought, he apologized for devoting so little attention to me.

"We sometimes forget the forest for the trees," was his way of putting it, "but I got so concerned with the questioning about Richard and Debbie that I forgot really to ask much about you, and I apologize for that. Are you still working as a real estate broker?"

"I have a license," I said.

"Are you actively pursuing your activities?"

"On a very limited basis."

"Do you still have the Greenway Realty business?"

"Yes."

"Do you still have an office out of which you do business?"

"No. I have an office out of my home now."

Once it had been established that my work schedule was extremely light, William Fox asked to what extent I had involved myself in real estate endeavors over the past six months.

"Since—since the accident I haven't been able to do much of anything," I told him. "I had some counseling myself."

"From whom?"

"Dr. Malone."

"Is he a psychiatrist?"

"Yes."

"Here in Phoenix?"

"And I have created a support group for other Flight 255 families. And I went to the Casa out here in Scottsdale. Jeannie Brand is the—it's a grief support group."

"At the present time you still live in the Moon Valley residence?"

"That's correct."

"Is your daughter with you now?"

"Yes. I asked her to move back in when Len—
because I didn't want to be in that house alone."

"And Christopher also?"

"Yes."

"Anybody else?"

"No."

"So—well, that's right, John's in Memphis and—
or James is in Memphis and John's in Sacramento,
correct?"

"Yes."

"You said that since Leonard's death you haven't
been able to do much of anything. Is that because of the
grief that you feel about it, or are you distracted? Or do
you know just why you have that feeling that you can't
do much of anything?"

"Well, I think it's a little hard to function when
your life has been destroyed."

Fox seemed altogether unconvinced of this. "I'm
trying to avoid being quarrelsome," he said. " 'You are
still alive' is the observation I was going to make, but
you have a feeling that your life has been destroyed
because of Leonard's death?"

"I'm trying to get by. I'm trying to put my life back together. But it's—Len was—Len was my life, and he's not here. I'm trying—I have to go in a whole new direction, and you know, when you're 20 or—you know, this is a very awkward age to be alone. I'm not young, I'm not old, and Len's not here. My whole life has changed because of this."

"Did you and Len have a circle of peers, friends, and acquaintances that you chummed around with when he was alive?"

"Yes, but mostly we chummed around with each other. We were never apart."

"Do you see any of those people on any regular basis?"

"It's not the same."

"I'm sure it's not. I just wondered if you maintained some contact with the circle of friends and acquaintances that you had during his lifetime."

"You see, when an accident like—everybody's there in the beginning."

"To offer their sympathy and condolences?"

"Yes, but ultimately you're alone."

"But I'm not sure you've answered my question,

so let me press on. Do you see any of those people who were among your circle of acquaintances before the accident took his life?"

"Yes."

"Do they have social events that you attend—dinners or anything?"

"I go out very infrequently. I spend my time with my children, and I go to church, and I write."

"You mean you write letters?"

"No, I write."

"As an author?"

"I write my thoughts down on paper."

"Did you maintain a diary during your marriage with Leonard?"

"No. No, this was after the accident I'm talking about."

"You began to write after that?"

"Yes."

"Leonard, as I understand it, had some hobbies. The one that sticks in my mind is that he was apparently a racquetball player."

"Yes."

"And he had, I guess, some other hobbies. They're

in the answers to interrogatories and it might be easier to look there, but off the top of your head, can you remember what other activities he engaged in?"

"Leonard played racquetball and that was confined to lunch hours at the bank, at the health club. Leonard was home at 6:00 o'clock every night. Leonard went skiing, but I went with Leonard, although I was a non-skier."

"Snow skiing?"

"Yes."

"Where?"

"Anywhere. Colorado, Flagstaff."

"Did you take regular ski trips?"

"No, not—he went a couple of times a year."

"Okay. What else?"

"The boat was really his main relaxation over in San Diego to get away."

"How often were you able to use that boat as a time-share participant?"

"Once a month. And oftener, if we wished."

"Did you get to San Diego once a month to utilize the boat, do you believe, on an average?"

"There would be some months we could not go for whatever reason."

"Did you utilize it for social purposes?"

"We went—we went to have some quiet time and be alone."

"Did you have friends and acquaintances among the other boat owners in the area where your boat was kept?"

"Not—we had—Larry Goertzen, who worked with Len at the bank, he and his wife would go with us, but not all the time."

"Did you utilize the boat for deep-sea fishing or . . ."

"No."

". . . for scuba diving or anything like that?"

"No, we didn't do that. We'd just go around the bay."

"What about your hobbies prior to the accident, other than—you worked quite a bit, I know, but aside from that, were you a skier or a crocheter or a bridge club member, or what sort of activities did you have?"

"I was very engrossed in my marriage and my children and my grandchildren and most of all Len, and he had asked me to cut back working so I'd be free to travel with him. He didn't want to leave . . ."

"Did he travel a good bit in his work?"

"Yes, quite a bit."

"Throughout the country or just throughout the state?"

"He wasn't gone every week, but he was gone several times a year and I can't—this Detroit trip was—I mean the New Jersey trip, that's one of the few times that we—we did not travel together."

"So your lifestyle has changed not so much because you have different activities that you now engage in, but simply because Leonard's not there to share your home and your life."

"My lifestyle has changed drastically, yes. I'm now alone. There's only one—me."

"How long has it been since you've seen the doctor, the counselor? What was his name?"

"About a month ago."

"What was his name, do you remember?"

"It wasn't a he. It was Dr. Malone—her."

"Oh, that's a lady."

"Yes, it is."

"Oh, okay. Do you have plans to see her again?"

"Yes, I do."

"Do you have an appointment?"

"No. I will see her at the end of summer."

"Do you go kind of on an as-needed basis?"

"Yes."

"And the grief support that you have organized, does that have . . ."

"That was the first—during the first year, and we had a memorial service and that's kind of served its purpose. It fulfilled a need at that time. I think we're all—we all want to try and get on with our lives, if possible."

"And then finally, you mentioned a group in Tempe that you had, didn't you?"

"No."

"I'm sorry."

"It was a grief support group that they have at the Casa, which is a Catholic . . ."

"That's what I'm thinking of. I thought it was in Tempe, but you were talking about the Casa."

"It's just a group, and it's for everybody. It's not the 255 group."

"I understand. And have you been an active participant in their meetings?"

"I was. I was the first year."

"At the moment you're just doing it on your own with an occasional assist from Dr. Malone, right?"

"And Father O'Carroll, yes."

"Thank you."

Once the deposition had ended, I reflected upon what the defense attorney had said about "forgetting the forest for the trees," as if my grief and loss meant nothing. He had sought to remind me of all the friends and activities I could still avail myself of. As if everything were essentially the same, if only I chose to see it in that light. His response to my contention that my life had been destroyed was that I was still alive—still breathing and functioning, in other words, as opposed to comatose or dead. I was astounded at his insensitive manner, his dismissal of my shattered life, that I should be grateful I was alive and in such pain. His unfeeling approach will be burned in my memory as long as I live.

I went away that day thinking that I had not explained myself very well. Quite possibly, such things could never be adequately explained. It was all too personal, too private for words. And words were all I had.

Driving home, it occurred to me that it wasn't always true that death was the end of everything, since there were times when it could just as easily be the start of a new and different kind of hell.

Chapter **6**

━━━━━━━━━━━

FOR A VERY long time, it did not occur to me to consider how my grief and overall dissatisfaction with life might be affecting friends of long-standing. While I was vaguely aware of their desire to be of some help to me, I could not imagine what I should possibly ask of them. Much later, I would hear myself described in ways that often surprised, even shocked me. In the process, I learned that my friends had suffered along with me during that tragic period following Len's death, and that their suffering, like mine, had been many-faceted.

Recently I discussed this with Carol, a friend for more than 25 years. She had seen me enter into various relationships that I subsequently terminated when they proved to be unfulfilling. Carol and I were working for the same real estate firm at the time I first met Len.

Her comments were: "It was obvious to me and everyone else who attended that party that the two of you were strongly attracted to one another the moment you met.

"He was special. And the two of you *together* were special. That was obvious from the first. Then too, he was exceptional in the sense that he never displayed any resentment toward your women friends, as husbands often will. I knew I was always welcome in your home, and that he was as happy to see me as you were."

"Yes," I said. "We complimented one another in all the right ways. And yet, it wasn't anything that either of us deliberately did. We just had this way of being whenever we were together."

"I thought of that on the day of the crash," Carol said. "I remember thinking that it wasn't possible that something had happened to him alone. By then, I always thought of the two of you together. I think everyone did."

"Yes," I said, "for a very long time, I lost all ability to function."

"I know," Carol said. "I was worried, too. There were those incredible periods of melancholy. And your inability to come to terms with things. I knew you weren't coping very well, and that you were harboring a great deal of bitterness and anger."

I nodded. "Yes. But that's only natural, isn't it?"

"For a time, it is. But it seemed to go on longer than it should have. Oh, I'm not trying to make less of Len's death. You mustn't think that. It's just that I longed for you to find an inner peace that I think is gradually coming to you now."

It was true that I had changed in certain ways, that I reacted somewhat differently now to all that had been lost. It wasn't resignation exactly, but more of an acceptance of those things that could never be changed.

"I think I feel calmer inside," I finally said.

"I know," Carol said. "You're more like the old

Rosie now, more like the Rose that Len once knew and loved."

It was a strange observation in that Len was no longer there to see how I looked and behaved, and yet, I often felt that he was.

"It's nice that you can remember him now in an easier, more pleasant way," Carol continued. "Without a sudden gush of tears."

"Except sometimes . . ."

"Yes, of course."

"It's still hard. I knew you were well-intentioned in suggesting that I do volunteer work, or anything at all in order to bring me out of myself."

Carol smiled. "I'm glad. I was never really sure if what I was saying or doing was the right thing for you. All I ever really wanted to convey was my willingness to be there for you."

"And you were. When I seemed to be the least aware of it, that's when I needed you most."

"I know you are writing a book about the crash. Has it helped you?"

"Yes. It's very therapeutic. However, I'm not

anyone famous—not anyone the reading public would be particularly interested in."

"It's the subject that people will identify with, Rose. Everyday, someone somewhere experiences the loss of a loved one, either through illness or through some other tragic occurrence. Think how they could benefit from all that you've managed to survive."

"It's an ongoing process, Carol. I don't really feel that I'm there yet."

"But that's just it. It's not something that can ever be erased or undone. It's something you learn to live with and, also, to live around. You develop coping skills, a new outlook, a different frame of reference in terms of your daily life. At the deposition you said that your life was over, and in a way, it's true. Your life with Len can never be again. But you still have a life. You're still a talented and vital person, someone who still has much to experience and share."

"But that's just the problem, you see, Carol. I can't seem to identify with that person—or that life. I've given it a lot of thought and what it really comes down to is that I'm not as self-sufficient as I once was. The reason is simple enough. I allowed myself to lean on

117

Len, to become increasingly dependent upon him for things I should have been providing for myself."

"Not necessarily," Carol said. "After all, he was there—and he wanted to care for you, to support you, and to be your buffer against the world."

"I know. But now he's gone. And the person I am without him has lost the knack for living independently. Maybe that's one of the basic differences between men and women. Women seem more inclined to immerse themselves totally in a relationship, to build their entire world around it, while men always hold something in reserve. Men have their careers, their professional associates and friends. I *used* to have those things, but they soon lost their value once Len came into my life. There's no doubt about it, Carol—Len would have survived this much better than I."

"Don't be too sure. With you he'd found a happiness he wasn't really expecting. The older we get, the more we tend to feel the odds are no longer with us."

"I know. By the time I met Len, the odds of meeting the right person, the only one for me—well, those odds were hardly in my favor. And yet it happened. Only to have him taken away in the most stupid and senseless way."

"I know," Carol said.

"If there are reasons for living, for *being*, mustn't there also be reasons for dying?"

"I'm sure there must be," Carol answered.

"It's understandable in cases where people are terminally ill," I said. "Or where some act of deliberate violence is involved. But I can't understand what happened to Len. It was preventable. No matter what they say or ever *try* to say about it, it was because of someone's carelessness and outright stupidity that this horrible thing happened. It didn't have to happen, and yet it did."

Leaning forward, Carol lightly patted my hand with her own. "There's something that Len used to say to you," she said, "something I actually *heard* him say one time when the three of us were together."

"What was that?"

"If anything ever happens to me—go for life."

"Yes," I immediately responded. "I remember him saying that."

119

"It was good advice, Rose."

"I know."

"At this point, I think he would want you to break away from all the old traditions, particularly at holiday time. I think he would prefer that you create some new traditions of your own, rather than constantly resurrecting the past."

"It hasn't really been possible to resurrect the past," I admitted. "In doing things the way they've always been done, I've had to face the fact that Len was an essential part of it all. It just doesn't work without him.

"Recently I had this dream. I dreamt I went home to Illinois and bought back the house I grew up in. I was in the process of remodeling it, when Len suddenly appeared. He asked if I intended to replace the foundation and the porches. I told him no, that I hadn't really planned on it. At that point, he insisted that I must—that nothing would work out unless I did that first."

"In other words, it's necessary to lay a new foundation. You can't build on the old."

"That's right."

"Well, there you have it, Rose. In the final analysis, it's the only logical thing. It isn't being disrespectful to Len to build on a new foundation. It's really all you can do."

It was true enough. I knew it as well as I knew that my life with Len could never be reclaimed, no matter how much I might wish for it to be so.

"You've been a good friend," I said to Carol, who continued to regard me with a certain amount of anxiety and concern. "If it sometimes seemed to you that I was fighting against the things you were saying, I want you to know that it wasn't really that. I know it hasn't been easy for you either."

"No, it hasn't," Carol admitted. "You're the first close friend I've ever gone through something like this with and grief is such a personal thing. In the end, we each have to handle it in our own way."

"You've made it easier for me just by realizing that," I said. "The kind of help and support you've provided have never been imposing. I just always knew it was there, if I needed it."

In saying this, it suddenly occurred to me that I had aptly described the very sum and substance of my friendship with Carol—all that it had ever been and would undoubtedly continue to be for as long as I was fortunate enough to have her in my life.

Another friendship that had spanned a period of 25 years by the time Len died was one that I shared with Sandy.

"It was obvious that he fulfilled your every need," she said. "I was so happy for you, Rose. After all the struggles you'd gone through raising three children on your own, after a number of unfulfilling relationships, and after finally reaching a point where you no longer believed there was anyone who would ever really understand you, or care for you—I know that Len must have seemed like a dream come true."

"He was," I told her. "And who would know better than you? After all, you and I were living in the same house at the time Len and I first met. I was always talking about him and seeing him constantly. The incredible thing about it is that I trusted him immediately—and because I did, I knew I had found someone truly exceptional."

"I knew it, too," Sandy said, "because of the way you were so totally focused on him. Right from the beginning. I kept thinking of various men I'd introduced you to before Len came along. You never seemed particularly interested in any of them."

"Until Len."

"I wish I had let him know how much I truly appreciated his friendship," Sandy said. "It's wrong to assume that a person already knows a thing like that. And even if they do—well, the words are still important."

In reflecting upon this, I knew I would always be grateful that Len and I had taken the time to express our feelings to one another. Through the years, we had somehow managed to retain the newness of our relationship. We had always been openly affectionate, constantly touching, and holding hands. And in the course of each day, Len would generally call me several times, if only to ask how I was. Knowing this, Sandy often said that if she could find another Len, she would be willing to remarry.

"I only vaguely remember the first time you visited me after the crash," I said. "At that time, I was determined to get a forensic report, which I hoped would prove that Len's body was actually not his body at all."

"I know," Sandy said. "I vividly remember that period of denial. For a very long time, there was simply no way of communicating with you. You were in such a state of anger and abject grief. And through it all, you kept asking how a thing like this could possibly have happened to someone as kind and good as Len."

"I still ask myself that," I said. "I know it's a pointless question in the sense that it can never change anything. Still, there's this persistent desire to know!"

Sandy nodded. "That's understandable. After all, the two of you created an extraordinary life together—one that was so much better than anything either of you had ever managed on your own. It seems so unfair that something like that could be lost."

"We were good together because we balanced each other out," I said. "Len was strong where I was weak, and vice versa. At the time I met him, I knew he was hurting. And searching. And trying to hold things together for his kids. I wanted to be there for him, in whatever way I could."

"And you were. Just as he was always there for you."

"That's right—he was. And I always thought he would be. So did he. Anytime I couldn't figure out some mechanical device around the house, he would tell me not to worry about it—that he would always be there to operate it. And I believed him, Sandy! I really believed *he would always be there.*"

"That's natural, I think."

"But then, when someone dies, it's like you've lost your own identity."

"And what about now?"

"What do you mean?"

"Now, I see you struggling to make annual holidays what they were when Len was still here. And, of course, that just isn't possible."

"I know."

"After a while, it's time to let go, Rose. Just like you did with the boat."

The boat. It had been a while since I'd thought about the boat—the way I'd continued to hang onto it, making monthly payments, fretting over its maintenance and

125

upkeep simply because Len had always enjoyed it. The boat had been *his* hobby, not mine.

Finally, I made myself dispose of it, along with a lot of other things.

"That first year, I tried to keep everything exactly as it had been before Len died," I reluctantly confessed. "I suppose that was my way of building a shrine to him. But only until you realized the futility in that. Time passes, Rose. Things change. *People* change. Even you."

"And you've come a lot farther than you think," she assured me. "You've begun to adapt to the way things are. There's not as much vacillation between the present and the past. And I think you've even started looking forward to the future now."

"In a way, I suppose I have," I said. "The future's still a major question in my mind, but I'm determined to find an answer."

Chapter 7

As TIME WENT ON, and my conversations with friends and family members continued, I realized how fragmented we had all become, each living through our individual perceptions of Len's death and what this loss actually represented in our lives.

How could I ever have imagined that I was totally alone in this? The suffering of others had been as real as my own. When I finally thought to ask, I found they were eager to speak of it.

My daughter Pam described conflicting emotions on the matter of how she should relate to me. "You seemed to want to be alone," she said. "You were so totally immersed in your grief. I wanted to help—to talk, to be there for you, but you seemed so far away."

In reality, I had wanted very much to be with others, to share what I was feeling and thinking, but the island of my isolation prevented me from reaching those I loved.

Now that the initial stages of grief had passed, I found it possible to talk more easily with Pam about those things we had most enjoyed and admired in Len.

I reminded her that she had once referred to him as a "keeper," that rare sort of man who, unlike so many others, was definitely worth keeping. From Pam's point of view, Len had proven to be the perfect counter-balance to my own volatile nature. While I had never heard it described in exactly that way, I knew I had always allowed myself to become too tense and distraught over inconsequential matters, something Len was never inclined to do. To the extent that he had always managed to calm me and supply a more logical perspective, I had been able to deal with daily problems in both a positive and effective way. That had been one of his gifts to me.

According to Pam, there had been one particular

quality in Len that made it extremely easy for her to relate well to him.

"It was the way he treated my friends," she said. "Not as if he were making an effort to get along with them, but as someone who truly did. He related well to people of all ages. His attitude toward teenagers was never condescending. He was outgoing and gregarious—and genuinely interested in whatever we were interested in. I remember how much he enjoyed playing ping pong with us. He was really enthusiastic, really competitive about the game."

Whenever Pam and I discussed Len, his relationship with Christopher inevitably entered the conversation. From the first, there had been a strong bond between Len and this child.

In one instance, when Pam found it impossible to locate a baby-sitter, Len offered to stay with the boy. Pam was initially hesitant since Christopher was still in diapers.

"Don't worry about it," Len insisted. "I know all about that stuff."

Actually, he hadn't known quite as much as he thought, for Pam later discovered Christopher wearing a diaper that Len had taped on him backwards.

Through the years, the two of them became extremely close, the boy working with joyful diligence beside his "Papa" as they picked grapefruit together or washed the car.

At the time of Len's death, Christopher was six years old. He listened with huge, somber eyes as Pam explained what had happened and why he would never see Len again. Somewhat uncharacteristically, the boy did not cry. He simply listened to all that was said and silently absorbed it. It was almost as if the tragedy itself had momentarily robbed him of his youth. Much later, he would reflect upon the many enjoyable experiences he had shared with Len, just as we all did, and I was relieved to see that he felt totally comfortable with these memories, that they did not seem to haunt him or cause him any anguish.

Among the more significant comments to come out of my discussions with Pam was her insightful observation that "when Len came along, he really came along for all of us." There was a great deal of truth in this, since everyone had clearly benefited from what he had to share. We were better and wiser for having known him. He had taught us by example, and now it was up to us to do the same. It was not enough to miss Len, to covet what we had experienced together, or even to reflect upon these experiences now and again. A major part of what he had given us needed to be passed on to others.

I thought of how my grandchildren might benefit from what their parents had learned from being children in a house where Len had once lived.

My son Jim had been given the gift of direction at a time when he was earnestly contemplating a career choice. Len suggested the computer field and even arranged for an entry-level position at the bank where he was employed. Once Jim became involved in computer programming, he could more fully appreciate the true potential and endless challenges that were now available to him.

By the time of Len's death, they had grown extremely close. How very difficult it must have been for Jim to lose the special relationship that existed between them. Still, because I was visiting him at the time of the crash, Jim's first concern was for me.

Jim and Richard later flew to Detroit to examine the personal effects of those who had died in the crash.

"Everything had been laid out on long folding tables," he later told me. "We were asked not to touch these items but to look at them carefully and see if we recognized anything. Small file cards had been placed in front of each item to indicate where it had been found."

According to Jim, the first thing he recognized was Len's wedding ring, an exact duplicate of my own.

He and Richard had arrived there with dental records with which they hoped to secure a positive identification. While they were there, however, no one ever asked them to view the body nor gave them any of Len's personal effects to bring back home.

Little was said after the two of them returned. We talked briefly and superficially. Afterwards, I remember that Jim called a doctor and asked that some sedatives be prescribed for me. From that point on, I spent most of my time in bed, conserving what little energy I had in order to prepare myself for the funeral. Once that was over, Jim returned to Memphis but continued to call every day.

Much of what we talked about at the time concerned itself with my inability to accept what had happened and the inevitable question of "Why?"

"I had no answers for you then and I haven't any now," Jim eventually admitted. "I only knew it was something you would gradually adjust to."

And he had been right. I know that now. The adjustment has been made, as well as it can ever be done. It has been made in the sense that my life with Len has finally been relegated to the past. I no longer have it confused with the present or seek to include it in my future. It is a beautiful memory now.

I knew that my children would be glad to know that I had finally progressed to this point after all that I had gone through, and all that they had experienced themselves. It has been a long and dreadful ordeal for all of us.

My son John had often referred to Len as "the only real Dad I knew." John had needed Len in his life for special reasons of his own. A high school student at the time, John needed a strong male influence in his life, someone to talk to, to attend sporting events with, someone to give him advice, and to help him in making major decisions. Len had done all these things, both willingly and well.

When he learned of the crash, John flew home from Denver and did all he could to assist in the final arrangements.

"Throughout that time," he later told me, "I felt as if I were moving in slow motion. None of it seemed real, or even possible. I kept waiting for it to end, as a play might end, but of course it never did."

Looking back on that time, I remember all the confusion and chaos concerned with those aspects of Len's death that John had willingly assumed. The funeral arrangements, the discussions with attorneys that inevitably led to the selection of Joseph Jamail, and finally, John's efforts to deal with my grief in the only way he knew how—to see to my needs, to determine what I wanted done, and to execute those acts in the best way he knew how.

Once it was finally over, John returned to Denver where family problems of his own began to preoccupy his time. During her seventh month of pregnancy, his wife miscarried a child. This tragic occurrence, along with the constant demands of his work, created some distance between us. Since we were already separated in a geographical sense, I found myself feeling even more lost and abandoned.

Overall, I know that my children are caring and supportive individuals, that they each felt a tremendous affection and respect for Len, and that they will always be grateful for what he contributed to their lives. In John's case, Len suffered through the typical period of teen-age rebellion. Matters on which they periodically disagreed eventually culminated in a major disagreement over a car. At the time, John already *had* a car that Len had bought him. It was a sensible, extremely reliable vehicle that John did not care for only because it was not at all "hip." Although he had been told not to do so, John traded the car in. The one he came home with was as sorry a specimen as any we had ever seen. From the outset, it required major repairs, and eventually, even caught fire.

One day, Len decided it was time for John to get another car. After dropping my son off at work, he made the rounds of the local car dealerships. He was driving John's car at the time. Suddenly, the police pulled him over and explained that the plates on the

135

car had expired. Len was ticketed, of course, which later caused another unpleasant scene at home. Still, there was an element of humor in it all that Len could always be counted on to see. Recalling his own youthful escapades perhaps, he was not inclined to be overly judgmental in matters of this kind.

Another interesting aspect of my marriage to Len was the closeness that developed between John and Len's son, Richard. In a situation where there might have been jealousy or resentment, there was instead great camaraderie. Richard also worked at the bank.

After the crash, he found it impossible to remain, finding it too painful to pass his father's office each day, which now sat vacant and still.

Len was extremely pleased with Richard's interest in aerospace engineering and proved highly supportive of this particular career choice. Ironically, it was a field that would later taunt Rich with its constant emphasis upon airplanes. Soon after Len's death, a course in accident investigation was offered to Richard, which he adamantly refused to take. Once he had explained to his advisor why he would never even consider such a class, nothing more was ever said about it.

At the crash site, Rich had already seen all he ever wanted to see of accident investigations. An odor permeated the air the entire time that he and Jim were there that was similar to the smell of irrigation water on a farm. Rich described it as a heavy, stagnant smell, which he eventually realized was the smell of human bodies.

As Richard and I began to share our feelings of pain and loss with one another, we gradually grew closer. It was a truly gratifying experience, and one that would later repeat itself with his sister, Debbie.

Debbie remembered Len as a supportive and caring father who always had his children's best interests at heart. Rather typically, Debbie had looked upon me as the "other woman" in her father's life. While these feelings had created a certain amount of strain between us, we had managed to work through them and, now, were finally able to enjoy one another, and openly and comfortably shared our fondest memories of Len.

As a family, it was obvious that we had gone

through both common and individual forms of grief. There were ways in which we felt closely bound by similar emotions, and other ways in which we grieved privately and alone. Overall, we are undeniably stronger as a family unit; certainly we are more empathetic toward one another's personal feelings and needs. Without question, we have learned a new language through tragedy, one that has not only taught us much but is teaching us still.

Chapter 8

MY DARLING LEN

I guess this book is my way of saying good-bye. It's a difficult thing to do, and yet I know it must be done.

The suit has finally been settled—three and one-half years after the crash. The manner in which it has dragged on, even as I have, is the ultimate absurdity.

I've come this far, primarily at the urgings of others who continue to insist that I must get on with my life. I'm told that I'm making progress and sincerely hope that this is true.

Len, I don't wish to be a burden to anyone, or even a source of concern. Friends and family have done what they can—now, I must do the rest.

I am determined to move ahead, taking occasional looks into the past. It is impossible to dismiss the past since, now and again there is that inevitable longing to look inside the self, to reflect in quiet moments upon so many cherished memories. To deny them is to deny their value, and that I could never do. It would be like sending the truth away.

What is the truth? Simply that you and I were meant for one another, and this can never be changed. I've now reached that place beyond grief that is sometimes difficult to explain or understand. It concerns itself not only with the finality of things but also with the reality of what we were, and must continue to be.

Is it building a shrine to you to insist that

140

you were an encounter in my life that can never be repeated? I think of it only as a fact.

Is it romanticizing the past to believe that what we shared was a truly unique experience, one that few people share or even know they have a potential for? Before we met, I could never have imagined the kind of life, the kind of love we were fortunate enough to know. Where did it come from? Not from you alone—nor from me alone. It was the combination of the two of us—whatever we were somehow able to awaken in one another—that caused all the rest of it to be.

Because of you, I no longer believe in coincidence. I know that there is a plan and an order to things, in the way people meet—and when. We met at a time when we were totally right for one another, having gained that quality of appreciation and gratitude that can only come with maturity and time. In my youth, it would have been easy to take so much for granted since that is the very essence of youth, to believe so devoutly in the constancy of things. In those early years, we cannot really envision an end.

The end, incidentally, is not what I thought it would be, since it is not an end at all. It is merely a rearrangement of daily occurrences and events, another road traveled, which earlier ideas, feelings, and experiences can quickly overshadow. Such is the nature of the past, which I realize now will periodically assert itself and make its own demands.

I've stopped fighting the past, just as I've stopped running from it. As a point of comparison, it is painful and difficult to endure. But as a reminder of total fulfillment, it invites the heart to continue to hope and believe.

A heart awakened to love remains somehow open to it, even after love itself has passed. I find that the magic and the miracle of it continue to enchant me. It all comes back in

142

songs I hear, in books I read, and, of course, through my private thoughts and dreams.

What do I dream about now? I dream about a world in which love is the dominant message and force. So much good has come out of the love you have given to others, Len. I see it in your children, in my children, and also, in myself. We are all richer and better for having known you. Our lives have been forever expanded because of your love. Because of you, we know something more about ourselves.

On a personal level, I know that I have evolved, that I have grown mentally, emotionally, and spiritually through my years with you, and that there is something that now needs to be done with what I have learned. I'm still working on that—trying to determine the best focus, the best way to convey what I've come to feel and know.

I often ask myself what YOU would do—how you would use what you have experienced through us in order to rebuild your own life, and possibly assist others in a similar situation.

It is my hope that this book might be of some comfort and help to those who have suffered the loss of a loved one, although I know that I'm still searching and that I've many more questions than answers.

From the first, I was determined to approach this book honestly, not offering any stereotypical approaches or so-called "pat answers," which could never really work for me. The fact is, I have been altered by all that has happened. My life is not the same. Its quality is changed, and there will always be this vacant spot where you once were. Still, it is a life. It has its own significance and meaning.

I often think about what I am here to contribute. In terms of this book, I'd like to be able to provide the proverbial "happy ending," but of course, that is impossible to do. Yet, the ending is not sad—it's merely incomplete.

Occasionally, I've tried to imagine someone else in my life, but that, too, is

Rose Weite

*impossible to do. For now, there is only your
face and all that we have shared together.*

*Another wedding anniversary will soon
be here, and as usual, Len, I'll be thinking of
you and missing you with all my heart.*

*I would like you to know that in one area
of my life, I've made considerable progress, and
that it concerns itself with the manner in which
I've chosen to regard pain. While memories can
indeed be painful, I have come to understand
that the pain itself is evidence that I'm still
alive. To live is to feel—and there is so much
that I do feel deeply.*

*In closing, let me say that I'll always
treasure what you and I have shared, and that
there is no material price that can ever be placed
upon such happiness. The court settlement
represented nothing more than what dis-
interested third parties chose to believe your life
(and death) were worth. As usual, they were
wrong.*

*My life with you was worth all that I am,
and all that I could ever be. Even if I had known*

145

beforehand how tragically it would end, I would do it all over again.

You have been the most wonderful experience, the finest and best thing that has ever happened to me. I will miss you all my life.

Sleep well, my love.

THE END AND THE BEGINNING

Epilogue

IN JUNE, 1991, the U.S. District Court ruled Northwest Airlines was at fault due to the flight crew's negligence, and the National Transportation Safety Board ruled the crash of Northwest Flight 255 was due to Pilot Error.

News sources:

August 17, 23 and 28, 1987 issues of The Detroit News